This JOURNAL Belongs TO:

Made in the USA
Coppell, TX
06 June 2024

33168546R00063